DRAMA WITH THE ELDERLY

DRAMA WITH THE ELDERLY

ACTING AT EIGHTY

By

FRED S. GREENBLATT, M.T.R.S.

Director of Activities
The Jewish Home and Hospital for Aged
Kingsbridge Center
Bronx, New York

Director of Dramatic Activities
Kittay House
Bronx, New York

CHARLES C THOMAS • PUBLISHER
Springfield • Illinois • U.S.A.

Published and Distributed Throughout the World by
CHARLES C THOMAS • PUBLISHER
2600 South First Street
Springfield, Illinois 62717

This book is protected by copyright. No part of it may be reproduced in any manner without written permission from the publisher.

© *1985 by* CHARLES C THOMAS • PUBLISHER
ISBN 0-398-05061-9
Library of Congress Catalog Card Number: 84-8896

With THOMAS BOOKS *careful attention is given to all details of manufacturing and design. It is the Publisher's desire to present books that are satisfactory as to their physical qualities and artistic possibilities and appropriate for their particular use.* THOMAS BOOKS *will be true to those laws of quality that assure a good name and good will.*

Printed in the United States of America
Q-R-3

Greenblatt, Fred S.
 Drama with the Elderly.

 Bibliography: p.
  1. Amateur theater. 2. Aged--Recreation. I. Title.
PN3156.G76 1984   792'.02   84-8896
ISBN 0-398-05061-9

This book is dedicated to:

The Kittay House Chorus and Players, who, for the past ten years as their director, have allowed me to enrich my life through their love, talent, and enthusiasm as elderly actors and extraordinary human beings.

PREFACE

THE person responsible for conducting the drama group in your facility has just left. You have been assigned (although you have no knowledge or previous experience with drama) to continue with the drama group as the director or coach. You may begin to ask some of the questions I asked when I found myself in the same predicament ten years ago. You may even believe in some of the folklore and myths that the aged person himself has been led to believe. How will I do this? Old people can't act! I'm sure they won't be able to memorize lines. They're always sick, complaining and lonely. Aging can't be altered, so what's the use of even trying! The aging are past their prime.

The sad part of these myths is that many, including the aged, truly believe in them. More importantly, as seen by Alex Comfort in his book, A Good Age, these myths as prevalent as they may seem, are not always easy to uncover. He points to the fact that other groups such as the Jews and Blacks who have been penalized by society, have lived with their prejudice all their lives. Some had the time to fight back, helping to build the basis for civil rights upon which others could benefit. However, the old realize they have become a minority only when they have become "old." By this time it may be too late. Society has already branded them as inadequate and unable to function as they did in their younger years.

The United States has made great strides in addressing the needs of older people. We have acknowledged the need for increased medical care, better housing and more food and clothing. However, the psychological and emotional needs of the aged still warrant a great deal of attention.

If this seems difficult to believe, visit a few of the places where old people live. Those who work with the aged in nursing homes and community centers witness the tremendous effects experienced by the many losses of the aged person, including one's spouse, friends or the physical ability to see or hear. Admission to a nursing home, no matter how good the facility may be, unfortunately adds to the old person's losses. Individuality and independence becomes difficult to achieve. The life of a nursing home patient becomes fragmented. The old person in many instances is almost forced to sit back while dietary provides their food, housekeeping changes their linens and the nursing department gives them their medications, only to name a few. The physicians often treat their ailments, ignoring their psychological and emotional need to be seen as a whole person. Professionals in the field of Geriatrics and Gerontology are witness to the effects of these physical and psychological losses on a daily basis. Growing *old* in America, becoming a nursing home patient or enrolling in the Golden Age club of the neighborhood senior center should not parallel the end of a meaningful life.

This book is intended for use by the Recreation Specialist, the Activity Director, the Social Worker or anyone who works with the elderly.

The quality and variety of recreation programs available in a nursing home, senior center or community organization, will depend upon its philosophy and objectives as well as its budget and available facilities. More important is the need for a qualified leader whose skills, imagination and self confidence will facilitate a positive approach toward achieving a successful recreation program. It is therefore the responsibility of the activity director to provide within these limits a meaningful and worthwhile program of activities.

Drama is one activity which through its positive approach and unending values will help bring a renewal of life's purpose back to this grossly neglected minority. Its invaluable benefits will help build a better self image, satisfying the basic psychological and emotional needs of the aged.

Sixteen years of experience in the recreation field has proven to me that many of us not only doubt the capabilities of the elderly, but we are unaware of the tremendous value drama holds for them. As a result, many of us are easily discouraged by the problems of instituting drama programs. In addition, little help is available and few books have been published, which further frustrates the recreation leader who may lack a background appropriate for use by a drama group.

Preface

This book attempts to provide the recreation professional with the necessary background, skills and assistance in setting up and implementing a successful drama program. The values and benefits of drama along with the variety of dramatic forms and scripts will be discussed. A complete step-by-step guide, including how to set up, implement and conduct a successful drama group will also be dealt with. Obstacles, such as memorization of lines and other physical problems, will also be discussed with some suggestions and techniques in helping to solve these problems.

Drama can be broken down into two broad categories: formal and informal. Informal drama is usually applied to those experiences in which ideas or stories are improvised and used without a formal script, including creative drama, story telling, role playing, skits and dramatic games. Formal drama are more highly organized elements of drama, usualy utilizing a script and performed for an audience. This usually includes musicals, puppet shows, pageants, comedy plays and dramas. Both forms are a valuable tool for the recreation director. However, since more literature appears to have been written on informal or creative drama, the focus of this book will be on formal dramatic activities. With this in mind, there will be included a general overview of informal drama as well as warm up exercises which can be used for any dramatic program.

Use this book as your own personal *script* or *guide* for creating a successful drama program. All of the techniques and skills utilized here, may be adapted to almost any level of the aged population. Don't be afraid to experiment. What works for you or your group, may not work for another.

Use this book as your basis for a solid foundation and build upon it to develop your own techniques and methods. Be creative and let your imagination help inspire a meaningful, enjoyable dramatic experience. The recreation leader who uses his own creativity, skills and imagination will not only help enrich the lives of his drama participants but will be rewarded in his effort as he helps re-establish the positive attributes of the older adult.

Fred S. Greenblatt

796 Bronx River Road
Bronxville, New York 10708

INTRODUCTION

DRAMA: A HISTORICAL PERSPECTIVE

ACTING has been defined as "an art or practice of representing a character other than oneself in the presence of an audience."[1] This may be accomplished through changing one's physical appearance, emotional expressions and speech or by using certain movements of the body. To this, one may add costumes, scenic effects or props, or one may wish to achieve his role through merely identifying with the character. Through this action and speech usually results a story or literary composition called Drama.

Acting or drama, which today may be considered a highly complicated art, may be traced back to the simple role playing games of children or to certain religious rituals formed among primitive societies.

Funk and Wagnalls, in their discussion of acting, note it was common that significant events related to the history of primitive tribes or societies were to be acted out through pantomime. Many tribes, while sitting around a communal fire, would reenact in pantomime a successful food hunt which may have recently taken place. Some tribal rituals included the use of costumes and masks to impersonate hunters searching for the animal. Worship and religious rituals were often *acted out* among such early cultures.

The first group to be considered professional *actors* were those of the ancient Greek Theatre. The Greek Theatre came about through primitive religious rites which honored the God Dionysus. During these rituals, a chorus sang hymns relating the story of the god and

---

[1]Funk and Wagnalls new Encyclopedia, 1975 ed., s.v. "Acting." p. 146.

other mythological heroes. Actors were later introduced, impersonating characters in the legends.

As Funk and Wagnalls point out, the origins of the history of drama, through the ancient Greeks, is almost immeasurable. Many of their classic plays are still performed. In addition, many words used in drama have their origins in the Greek language. "The word "drama" itself is Greek, and such terms as "theatre," "scene," "thespian," and "proscenium" are derived from the Greek."[2]

To understand the birth of drama is to appreciate one of the oldest and most precious art forms of human life. To preserve this art form allows us to become a link of civilization which helps bridge the cultural heritage of every generation. As Howard Danford states:

> "One of the greatest challenges to the recreation leader is to convey the best of our cultural heritage to the present generation, thus strengthening the ties that bind our civilization to the great civilizations of the past, and to preserve all that is of cultural value for them in our own."[3]

DRAMA AND RECREATION

To open the curtain on dramatics as a recreation activity, is to spotlight an arena enriched with more opportunities for personal fulfillment, growth and enjoyment that almost any other existing art form.

Among the values and benefits of drama, as a recreation activity, is the renewal of self confidence and feeling of accomplishment which comes about through exhibiting talent, skill or intellectual capabilities. The ability to perform, memorize lines or take on the role of another character, increases one's self image and maintains mental activity. Participation, whether it involves acting on stage or assisting behind the curtain, provides enjoyment and a purpose in life. Further, belonging to a *special group*, and working together as a *team*, brings a certain status to the participant. Self expression and emotional outlet also add to he satisfaction gained through the dramatic

---

[2]Ibid., p. 148.
[3]Howard G. Danford, *Creative Leadership in Recreation* (Boston: Allyn and Bacon, Inc., 1964), p. 276.

arts. Finally, dramatics benefits the audience as well. Successful performances by the elderly provide not only an enjoyable recreation experience, but sometimes inspires others to join the drama group.

Drama has so much to offer in such a variety of ways; almost anyone can participate in this recreation activity. The varying types of participants make it possible to cast so many different roles. Since acting is so easily adaptable, people of all degrees of health may participate.

The emphasis in recreational drama is on the individual rather than the performance itself. The significance of dramatics is not what the person can do for the drama but what the drama can do for the person in providing a satisfying and meaningful experience.

With the emphasis on the individual, the director has an even greater challenge in achieving the best possible performance. However, a good performance will more than likely occur when the positive attitude and proper philosophical approach of the recreation leader outweighs the importance of the final production.

ACKNOWLEDGMENTS

"No man is an island entire of itself"
John Donne
Devotions upon Emergent Occasions
(1624) #17
"No Book Stands Alone"

I WOULD like to acknowledge with grateful thanks and appreciation the following people who either personally or professionally have in their own way contributed to the writing of this book.

First, to the Administration of The Jewish Home and Hospital for Aged, Kingsbridge Center, whose constant support and encouragement have been instrumental to the success of our drama group.

To the Director of Kittay House, Mrs. Beatrice Lewis, and her wonderful staff, who have been a motivating force and part of our drama group family since its inception.

To Esther Bialo, Kittay House tenant, and her talented assistants, who have designed and constructed the lavish costumes for all of our productions.

To my favorite eighty-four year old volunteer, Nathan Charney, whose wisdom, brilliance and guidance has taught me once again the true value of the "older" person.

To my special friend and colleague, Dr. Miriam Lahey, who has been a guiding light and inspiration to my personal and professional growth as both a recreation educator and a human being.

Finally, to my wife and three sons, without whose unselfish love, support and patience, this book would never have become a reality.

Special thanks to the activity leaders and drama coaches of the of the following facilities who have taken the time and effort to complete the drama survey utilized in gathering some of the pertinent information and statistics incorporated into this book.

Beth Abraham Home and Hospital
Bronx, New York

Bezalel Health Related Facility
Far Rockaway, New York

Brandywine Nursing Home
Briarcliff Manor, New York

Briar Crest Nursing Home
Ossining, New York

Cabrini Nursing Home
Dobbs Ferry, New York

Cobble Hill Nursing Home
Brooklyn, New York

Concourse Nursing Home
Bronx, New York

Daughters of Jacob Geriatric Center
Bronx, New York

East Haven Health Related Facility
Bronx, New York

Florence Nightingale Nursing Home
New York City, New York

Forest View Nursing Home
Forest Hills, New York

Freidwald House
New City, New York

Golden Gate Health Related Facility
Staten Island, New York

Hillside Manor Health Related Facility
Jamaica, New York

Lincoln Square Home for Adults
New York City, New York

Long Island Nursing Home
Jamaica, New York

Menorah Home and Hospital for Aged
Brooklyn, New York

Mermaid Manor Home for Adults
Brooklyn, New York

White Plains Center for Nursing Care
White Plains, New York

Workmans Circle Home for Aged
Bronx, New York

CONTENTS

	Page
Preface	vii
Introduction	xi
Drama — A Historical Perspective	xi
Drama and Recreation	xii
Acknowledgments	xv

Chapter One. THE VALUES AND BENEFITS OF DRAMA 3
  Feeling of Accomplishment 3
    A Positive Self Image 4
  A Purpose in Life 4
  Working as a Group 5
    A Team Approach 5
  Emotional Outlet and Creative Self Expression 6
  Meaning for the Audience 7
Chapter Two. DRAMATIC FORMS AND SCRIPTS 10
  INFORMAL DRAMA 10
    Creative Drama Improvisation 10
    Story Telling 11
    Dramatic Games 11
    Pantomime 11
    Choral Speaking 11
    Movement Activities 12
  FORMAL DRAMA 14
    Puppet Shows 14

Bag Puppets	14
Styrofoam Puppets	15
Pageants	15
Original Scripts	16
Existing Scripts	17
Adaptations of Existing Scripts	17

Chapter Three. FORMING A DRAMA GROUP 20

Essential Components 20
The First Step 22

Chapter Four. CONDUCTING A SUCCESSFUL DRAMA GROUP 24

Purpose of the Group 24
Initial Meeting Time 24
Selection of a Show 25
Adapting the Script 25
Auditioning 26
Rehearsals 27
PRODUCTION AIDES 27
   Costumes 28
   Make-up 28
   Scenery 28

Chapter Five. MEMORIZATION OF LINES 31

Memory Studies—Implications for Drama 32
Memorization Aides and Techniques 34
Supportive Environment 35
Interference 36
Other Helpful Hints 36

Chapter Six. THE ROLE OF THE DIRECTOR 38

Creating a Positive Atmosphere 38
Achieving Change 38
Attitude of the Director 40
Dealing with Health Problems 40
Dealing with Personality Problems 43
   The Passive Participant 43
   The Assertive Participant 44

Table of Contents xxi

    The Negative Participant 44
    The Director as Producer 45
    Humor and the Director 45
Chapter Seven. INTEGRATING DRAMA WITH OTHER
    PROGRAM AREAS...................................... 46
APPENDIX I.   "THIS-THEY CALL A CHICKEN?" –
                  AN ORIGINAL COMEDY. 48
APPENDIX II.   DRAMA GROUP ASSESSMENT AND
                  INTEREST QUESTIONNAIRE 56
APPENDIX III. DRAMA SURVEY 58
APPENDIX IV. SUGGESTED MATERIALS FOR ELDERLY
                  DRAMA GROUPS 64

Bibliography 67

DRAMA
WITH THE ELDERLY

CHAPTER ONE

THE VALUES AND BENEFITS OF DRAMATICS

Feeling of Accomplishment

A SIGNIFICANT value of drama is the feeling of accomplishment one achieves through the process of participation in a purposeful activity.

Success in memorizing lines (see Chapter Five), acting for the first time and standing in front of an audience provides the participant with a tremendous feeling of pride and accomplishment. This feeling of accomplishment undoubtedly results in an increased self confidence, self esteem and positive self image.

Dr. Dennis E. Waitley believes our self image determines the kind of person we are. We see ourselves and create our own self image based upon every thought, triumph or loss we experience. Every event in our environment and our lives contributes to the development of our self image.

According to Dr. Waitley, the self image is the fundamental key to understanding human behavior. "It is not what you are that holds you back, it is what you think you are not."[1] Dr. Waitley believes individuals behave not in accordance with reality, but in accordance with their perception of reality. How an individual feels about himself is the most important part of his self image and life. For all anyone does or wishes to do in life is based upon his self concept.

---

[1] Dr. Dennis E. Waitley, *The Psychology of Winning — Positive Self Image*, Tape No. 3, (Chicago: Nightingale-Conant Corp., 1978).

Old people who are told they are useless by society will believe they are useless, resulting in a decreased ability to function. Thus, the older person who feels he can not do anything, perceives himself as *old and useless* and is therefore unable to act. A negative mental picture of our self image, begins to control us, thereby making it difficult to outgrow the limits we place upon our self.

A Positive Self Image. To achieve a positive self image, we must therefore set new limits in a positive self direction. Thus, changing one's self image will facilitate a change in one's personality and behavior.

> "Dramatics permits renewal of self confidence because it enables an older adult to exhibit talent, skill or intellectual capability that may be overlooked during the normal course of social interaction."[2]

Drama affords elderly participants the opportunity to use their abilities, gaining recognition and helping to change their self perception. With an increased feeling of accomplishment, the older person is able to set new limits for himself, thereby achieving a more positive self image. The completion of a successful dramatic production is so often echoed with the comments: "I never knew I could do it." "I feel like a new and useful person."

A Purpose in Life

Dramatics is an important vehicle which provides its participants with a purpose in life and a common goal to work toward. Its value as a worthwhile recreation activity gives the elderly something to look forward to. Weekly rehearsals and the anticipation of a finished production give the elderly a chance to become involved in a pleasurable and meaningful experience.

The importance drama has played to the elderly has been evidenced by several drama groups. One drama coach recalls an eighty-year-old participant who had to have emergency laser beam treatments on her eye the same day her play was scheduled to be held at her facility. Refusing to miss her opportunity of being on stage, she

---

[2]Jay S. Shiver and Hollis F. Fait, *Recreational Service for the Aging*, (Philadelphia: Lea and Febiger, 1980), p. 160).

took a taxi from her physician's mid-town office to the home and arrived one hour before the show began. Another coach remembers an eighty-two year old woman who had a breast cancer operation. Three weeks after the operation, she was back on stage refusing to relinquish the leading role in her production.

Working as a Group

Another important value drama brings to its elderly participant, is the opportunity of working together as a group. Drama by its very nature offers the opportunity of participation at several levels within the group situation or process. Dramatics allows its participants to act, draw scenery, become a stage hand or prop person, design and create costumes or help with programs and publicity. Its diversity allows for participation on every level regardless of the elderlies' physical and/or psychological limitation. Often, the physically disabled have psychological problems resulting from their handicaps. For example, a blind or deaf person may be withdrawn and isolated from his peer group, making his role in society uncertain. The group process facilitates communication among its members, increasing social interaction and distinguishing a more significant role for the individual within society.

A Team Approach. Working as a cooperative team, also helps instill a greater feeling of respect and acceptance among its members. Those who forget a line may need to be helped by their fellow actors. The level of patience and tolerance is increased as everyone works toward a common goal. Self criticism and problem solving become acceptable in a positive way which would probably otherwise not occur.

> "Cooperation, responsibility and loyalty to a common enterprise gain new importance as the performers learn that even the star of the show cannot shine successfully if the "bit" player forgets his cue. Drama gives a maximum of opportunities for conditioning attitudes and group reaction and for developing imagination."[3]

Finally, as Richard Kraus states, "the group experience is an intensive, demanding one, and the members of the group learn to

---
[3] R.E. Carlson, T.R. Deppe and J.R. MacLean, *Recreation in American Life*, 2nd Edition, (Belmont, California: Wadsworth Publishing Company, 1972), p. 435.

develop individual responsibility, sensitivity and both leadership and fellowship."[4]

Emotional Outlet and Creative Self Expression

Another invaluable benefit of dramatics is the opportunity for emotional outlet and creative self expression of the participant.

Drama gives the participant a chance to play roles, express emotions and ventilate fear and hostilities through a socially acceptable channel. An elderly actor may be asked to exhibit anger on stage because of the role he is required to play. Although he may be directing his anger at someone on stage, his real feelings may be related to someone else in his life. The role he plays allow him to express his innermost feelings in a way that is acceptable and even applauded by the audience. In addition, as Richard Kraus points out:

> "Drama, because it is make believe, provides a vehicle through which he can safely express himself, making his feelings and needs known to others through which he can temporarily leave his own identity to play other roles."[5]

In playing another role, the actor must study the character's behavior and actions. He may therefore acquire a better understanding of people and a deeper sense of sympathy through an analysis of the character and his situation. The actor may also become exposed to a role of character he has never played before. Martin Nolter, in The Gerontologist, explains that:

> "in relating to other characters in a play, a person becomes highly aware of the feelings of that person in his character. This too, is extended to one's personal life and focuses upon his perception of others."[6]

He continues to point out that:

> "The satisfaction of discovering in oneself the emotions, the re-

---

[4]Richard Kraus, *Recreation Leaders Handbook*, (New York, Toronto, London: McGraw-Hill Book Company, 1955), p. 223.
[5]Richard Kraus, *Therapeutic Recreation Service — Principles and Practices*, 2nd edition, (Philadelphia: W.B. Saunders Co., 1973), p. 136.
[6]Martin Nolter, "Drama for the Elderly: They Can Do It," *The Gerontologist*, Vol. 13 No. 2, (Summer, 1973), p. 153.

sponses and the attitudes that are a part of a character one is creating is a personal response that makes one aware of the feelings in one's everyday life."[7]

The increased awareness in one's life and the opportunity of seeing the world or a particular character in a different perspective may also help to break down the barriers of prejudice. R.E. Carlson feels:

"A sense of dramatic is as necessary for enriched living as a sense of humor. Child and adult enjoy the release of being someone else, if only for a few moments, and the vicarious thrill, the empathy of identifying with others who are performing can bring as great a pleasure."[8]

Meaning for the Audience

An additional benefit of dramatics is the meaningful experience it holds for the viewing audience, especially the elderly. Not only does drama provide a pleasurable form of recreative entertainment to its audience, but it facilitates an increased self confidence among those watching their peer group on stage. The successful production and recognition of the actors becomes a positive influence on the audience, sometimes inspiring others to join the drama group.

As much publicity as possible should be given to the final production, since dramatics stresses the positive attributes of the elderly so well.

A special performance can be held for friends and family members of the cast. Other nursinghomes and community centers can also be invited. If the group is well enough and ambulatory the show can be taken *on the road*.

I can recall the exciting experience of taking our musical production to a joint campaign-fund raising luncheon of the United Jewish Appeal and Federation of Jewish Philanthropies. A group of one hundred women, whose minimum donation had to be $500.00 to attend, were present. One of the reasons for inviting our elderly drama group was to show how the monies distributed by UJA-Federation were being used in nursing home facilities such as ours.

---
[7]Ibid., p. 153
[8]Carlson, Deppe and MacLean, *Recreation in American Life*, p. 432.

Figure 1. Wheel chair resident of elderly drama group, enjoying emotional outlet and creative self expression in portrayal of character from musical production.

The group gave such an awe-inspiring performance, that several ladies jumped up, pledging additional donations. By the end of the day, the drama group helped raise almost eight hundred thousand dollars in donations. Not only did the group receive a special award of thanks and appreciation, but they went home with a feeling of pride and accomplishment which far exceeds any monetary value. Finally, their performance helped further break the myth of aging to their captive audience.

The media is another excellent way to help publicize and recognize the positive values of the elderly through drama. As Alex Comfort writes, there is so much bias against the elderly because "like racism, which it resembles, it is based on fear, folklore and the hang-ups of a few unlovable people who propagate these."[9]

Whenever possible, we must use every tool at hand, to help break down the barriers of prejudice. The media is an important tool and should be used whenever we have the chance to educate the public at large who the elderly really are. The media "can greatly influence attitudes, both by showing the old what age could be, and by disabusing the community at large what age is."[10]

---

[9]Alex Comfort, *A Good Age*, (New York: Crown Publishers, Inc., 1976), p. 35.
[10]Ibid., p. 132.

CHAPTER TWO

DRAMATIC FORMS AND SCRIPTS

As previously mentioned, drama may be broken into two broad categories: informal and formal. Although this chapter will focus mainly upon a variety of forms and scripts appropriate for use with formal dramatic activities, it is necesary to discuss briefly the importance of informal drama as well.

INFORMAL DRAMA

Informal drama is usually ascribed to those who enjoy participating in drama utilizing ideas, events or stories which may be improvised through action and dialogue without a formal script. Those who enjoy informal drama are usually less concerned with acting itself than they are with enjoying a creative, emotional experience. Informal drama includes creative drama, story-telling, dramatic games, pantomime, choral speaking and movement activities.

Creative Drama-Improvisation

Ideas or stories may be developed through using one's own imagination and personal experiences. The drama is improvisational and scripts are rarely used. The emphasis of Creative Drama is to share an experience for one's own enjoyment, rather than for an audience. Scenery and costumes are substituted by one's imagination and emotional feeling of a certain situation.

Story-Telling

Story-telling usually involves reading or telling a story (be it fact or fiction), to elicit some kind of emotional response. Songs can be used to help express the dramatic dialogue. Stories can also be told in which a small group or audience follows or imitates the actions of the leader. The *Lion Hunt* is a favorite story for informal drama. The leader sits facing his participants in a circle and asks if they want to go on a Lion Hunt. He pantomimes a story of looking for a lion. As he claps his hands at different tempos, while pantomiming the story, his audience tries to follow him. These kinds of stories help stir one's imagination while eliciting emotional responses.

Dramatic Games

These may include quiet or active games, many originating from folk customs or ceremonial rituals. Such games include *charades* or *New Orleans*. Singing games such as *Blue Bird, Blue Bird, Through my Window*, can also be fun. These combine songs and drama which are sung and acted out by the participants.

Pantomime

Pantomime is a form of drama which utilizes the body to express thoughts and actions. This form of creative drama may be engaged in purely for relaxation or recreation purposes. Pantomime such as *charades* are an excellent warm up game and have a social recreational value for its participants. A good way of using pantomime is for the leader to ask its group members to say as many things as they can without using their voice. Some may pantomime that they are hungry, sleepy, happy or sad. Participants can later be asked to describe a specific scene or situation. A further step could include emotional expression and characterization of some one different than ourselves.

Choral Speaking

A type of semi-dramatic activity; this dramatic form utilizes the voice without the need for participants to actually act on stage. This type of drama requires the reading of poetry, or prose, and can also encompass the use of songs. The prose or poetry is usually arranged in a logical order, telling some kind of story.

Dramatic readings are especially appropriate for holiday programs and can be used for events such as Thanksgiving, Christmas or George Washington's Birthday.

This type of activity is an excellent way of beginning a newly formed drama group. Participants need little experience to be part of a dramatic reading or choral speaking group, yet it helps develop a group discipline and cooperative effort. It also helps break the barrier of speaking before an audience, without the pressure of having to act or memorize lines as in a formal production.

Some caution should be used when participating in a dramatic reading. The elderly should be taught how to hold their scripts while maintaining eye contact with the audience. Microphones should be used in case the person's script muffles their voice area.

Movement Activities

Another excellent warm up tool is the use of movement activities. Exercise and movement usually involves the total body which helps raise the energy level and respiration and stimulates bodily circulation.

Exercises are an excellent means of improving bodily movement. Lindner and Caplow, in their book, Therapeutic Dance Movement suggest:

> "To increase the movement range and abilities of the aged individual, encourage them to extend and flex their bodies in as many different directions as possible. The use of the natural rhythm of swinging, in which the weight of the body gives in to the pull of gravity, develops balance and provides the experience of the interaction between control and release."[1]

The authors also suggest eight basic actions devised by Rudolf Laban in his "Effort Shape Method" and Audrey Wethered in "Movement and Drama in Therapy." These actions provide a good variety for warm up exercises and creative activities:

---

[1] Erna Caplow Lindner, Leah Harpaz and Sonya Samberg, *Therapeutic Dance Movement*, (New York: Human Sciences Press, 1979), p. 76.

Dramatic Forms and Scripts 13

Figure 2. Drama group presenting their dramatic reading, "A Visit with President Lincoln and Washington." An excellent beginning for a newly formed drama group.

1. Thrusting (hammering and punching)
2. Pressing (pushing and pulling)
3. Wringing (unscrewing a tight jar lid)
4. Slashing (cutting wheat or cracking a whip)
5. Flicking (brushing off dust)
6. Dabbing (patting or powder)
7. Gliding (smoothing a tablecloth or ironing clothes
8. Floating (moving like a feather in a breeze)[2]

Warming up the body is an important activity which makes one more aware of the space around him, adding a sense of freedom and control to the individual. A complete description of exercise progressions which may be helpful to the drama leader can be found in Lindner and Harpaz' book, Therapeutic Dance Movement.

---

[2]Ibid., p. 259.

Informal dramatic activities, especially creative drama are useful as warm up tools for any drama group. Because creative drama facilitates emotional responses and creative expression, without the use of a script, it is a good way to create an atmosphere conducive to the dramatic club. Once the participants become more at ease through creative drama, the groups' transition to formal dramatic activities will be smoother.

FORMAL DRAMA

This type of drama is more highly organized and is intended to be acted out by its participants in front of an audience. Costumes, scenery, makeup and lighting effects usually accompany these types of scripts. A variety of dramatic scripts are available for use by elderly drama groups. The following are some forms commonly used.

Puppet Shows

Although puppet shows are seldom used with elderly groups, they are appropriate for beginners since it requires no memorization of lines. They also allow the participant to become involved without acting on stage or facing the audience. Puppet shows provide good outlets for emotional expression, giving the participant the opportunity of taking on the personality of the puppet. It also provides the participant with the chance of making puppets which can be fun.

This type of dramatic form is especially appealing to children and is successfully used with them as the audience.

A variety of puppets can be used, depending upon the participants and the audience.

Bag Puppets. Ordinary paper bags can be easily made into interesting hand puppets. Faces can be drawn on the bags or cut out and pasted on the bag. Features such as hair, eyebrows, etc. can be added with ribbon, felt or yarn.

If you are lucky enough to have an artist or art specialist on your staff, you can have him draw or paint the faces of your drama participants and paste them on a bag. A puppet show, using your own drama group participants as the characters, will help provide hours of fun. Discussions centered around their past lives, or their life at

Figure 3. Bag puppet.

the nursing home, can be conducted with the puppets. This type of puppet show is especially useful with the more regressed patient and can also be used in conjunction with a reality orientation group.

The paper bag puppet can also be stuffed with newspaper or another material. Adding a stick and tying it closed makes another type of puppet. These puppets are easily made and provide a good means for discussion of little plays or skits. All of these puppet shows provide an excellent tool for the deteriorated patient.

Styrofoam Puppet. Using round balls of styrofoam, a variety of puppets can be made. Decorate the face with felt or oak tag, cutting into desired shapes for eyes, nose, hair, etc. Stick the shapes into the styrofoam with paper fasteners or tooth picks. Hats can also be made for the top of the styrofoam. Wooden dowels or pencils covered with material or tin foil can be inserted for movement of the puppet.

Pageants

Pageants have proven to be an appropriate dramatic form for beginners since the participant usually does not have to speak. One or two people can narrate while others act out the narrative being read.

Pageants are useful for holiday shows and fashion shows. They provide a good stimulus for new actors who do not have to memorize lines, yet are provided with audience exposure.

Figure 4. Styrofoam puppet.

Original Scripts

Original scripts can be fun but are often difficult to write. An original script should be a story or event familiar to the participant who will be acting.

This type of script is a good way to involve the participants directly. Participants can relate their own individual story focusing upon a particular event which they have shared at some point in their life. The story can also be written around events in which the participants are presently involved. Those who write their own script and create their own material tend to remember their lines more easily, since they are familiar with what they will be acting.

After several years of utilizing existing scripts, our drama group decided to try a hand at writing an original script. Our play centered around the experiences of the dining room in their apartment house residence for senior citizens. One member related an experience of her table mate who was never satisfied with the food she was served, especially the chicken. Always complaining about the black lines in her uncooked chicken, she exclaimed: "This you call a chicken, this is no chicken, this is a rooster!" A three act play was written around this experience (see Appendix I).

Any drama leader who writes an original script should be familiar with the basic elements of a play or story. They should be concerned with the characters, the story line and plot or climax.

Existing Scripts

Probably, the most popular dramatic form used by drama groups with the aged, is the existing script or an adaptation of such a script.

Most elderly people enjoy and relate best to musical scripts or shows, since they are familiar to them and are usually free of violence. Many Broadway plays can be suitably adapted for use with the elderly. Musicals such as "My Fair Lady," "Annie Get Your Gun," "Oklahoma," "Showboat," "Fiddler on the Roof," and "Hello Dolly," have proven to be appropriate for use by the aged actor.

Adaptations of Existing Scripts

Existing scripts can be adapted in several ways:

1. The entire script can be cut in length by rewriting the play, using the basic story line in shorter form. Only the most popular songs can be used if desired.
2. Certain scenes or acts can be totally eliminated by using a narrator to tell the story in much shorter form.
3. Changing the location of the play may make the production more realistic, making it easier for the elderly members to relate to. For example, a drama group in a Jewish nursing home wanted to put on "My Fair Lady." However, the director felt if Eliza Doolittle was a poor Jewish girl from the lower east side trying to learn English, the actors would relate more easily to the story line and the play. Thus, Eliza Doolittle became Eliza Dubinsky, a poor Jewish girl from the lower east side, struggling to become a lady, learning to rid herself of her yiddish accent, and native tongue. The play proved to be a great success to the aged actors as well as to their audience.
4. The time or date the story takes place can also be changed to meet the needs of the drama group. The same characters of an existing play can be used in a story which takes place a decade or even a century later or earlier.

5. A common problem to many elderly drama groups is the lack of male participants. Existing scripts can be rewritten, leaving out certain male roles or by changing a male role to a female role. The director must be careful, however, not to change the story line or plot if roles are reversed. Some groups have also utilized successfully their female members who took on a male role.

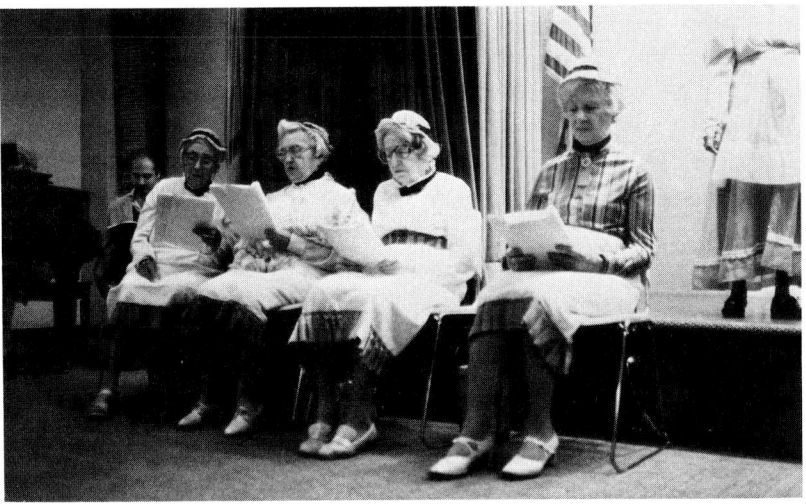

Figure 5. Female participant of drama group portrays *male* role in a musical production.

6. Some plays have scenes or acts which can be presented independently. The use of a narrator is effective in this case, describing the rest of the play.
7. The use of a chorus is an excellent means of including all members in a dramatic production. The chorus members add to the musical numbers and give those who don't want a large part the chance to participate in the group.

While adapting any script, the drama leader should remember that no actor should have too long a part or too many lines to memorize. Since it is often difficult to acquire understudies, the script should not depend too much on any one character in case they are forced to leave the show due to illness or death.

Finally, the drama leader should remember that before utilizing

Figure 6. Chorus of elder's drama group add to the musical score of the group's production.

an existing script, written permission from the author or publisher is necessary. In certain cases, a small fee may also be required for use of the script.

CHAPTER THREE

FORMING A DRAMA GROUP

Essential Components

CERTAIN components are essential in forming and setting up a drama group. Often, the lack of these components seems to contribute to those who have been unable to form their group successfully. The results of an informal survey taken by the author (see Appendix III), are discussed below. Questionnaires were sent to fifty nursing homes and twenty-five responses were received. The following table lists some of the components most commonly seen as necessary to the formation and establishment of a successful drama group. Also listed are suggested ways to obtain these necessary ingredients. Some of these have also been found in senior centers and residential care settings as cited by Paula Gray in her book "Dramatics for the Elderly: Guide for Residential Care Settings and Senior Centers."

Table I

ESSENTIAL COMPONENTS IN FORMING A DRAMA GROUP

Essential Component:	*Means of Achieving Component:*
Drama Coach.	Activity director or activity leader can form group and lead members.
	Seek volunteers with experience in drama or music.

Table I (Cont'd.)

Essential Component:	Means of Achieving Component:
Basic or Simple Knowledge in Dramatics.	Contact local college or high school drama or music department. Contact local "Y" when available. Read books on drama or recreation which may be available in library. Utilize basic recreation and music skills when available. Utilize skills acquired in training workshops. Utilize experience, ideas and knowledge of participants. Develop own style with members.
Appropriate Dramatic Material.	Use public library for possible resource of dramatic material. Write own script, using past experiences or events of participants.
Adequate Funds.	Apply for a grant to local bank or other community resource. Ask for donations of materials for use of costumes. Use plays requiring minimal props and settings. Use scraps and disregarded household items for props and scenery when needed.
Proper Facilities. Adequate Space.	Use dining room. Rent portable platform or have the engineering department in your facility build a small portable stage. Create a circular stage. Put chairs in a circle with stage in middle.

Table I (Cont'd.)

Essential Component:	*Means of Achieving Component:*
Adequate Interest of Drama Participant.	Encourage client to attend even as an observer at the beginning. Use warm up exercises or improvisations to stimulate interest. Publicize success of previous shows in resident newspaper.
Adequate Self Confidence of Participant.	Clarify the purpose of the drama group. Emphasize the importance of enjoying drama as a meaningful recreation experience rather than trying to achieve a certain level of success with the production. Schedule sufficient rehearsals to increase self confidence. Provide continued positive reassurance and constant praise. Give productions to appreciative audiences. Invite friends and relatives. Arrange for as much publicity as possible.

The First Step

For those who do not have an existing drama group, the following suggestions may also be considered in setting one up.

- Send a notice to all residents, inviting them to a meeting to help them begin a drama group. Be sure to note that no acting experience is necessary to be part of the group. Emphasize that anyone is welcome to join. Be specific in noting that there will be a job for everyone, including acting, stage hands, costume making, scenery painting, publicity and others.
- Post notices throughout the facility on all patient floors and bulletin boards.
- Announce the meeting of the drama group in the dining rooms, at resident council meetings and at any other place the residents meet.

Alert activity leaders may notice the potentials of certain residents by observing them at sing-a-longs or other recreation activities where they may stand out. Take note of those who are already active in recreation programs and who may exhibit outgoing personalities. Look for those residents who enjoy speaking at resident functions or public events. You may also know residents who have written articles for the resident newspaper. They may enjoy helping to write an original script. Try approaching those residents who participate in arts and crafts. They may wish to become involved in painting scenery for shows or drawing program covers or even helping with props.

For those residents who seem hesitant to attend, a bit of encouragement may be necessary. Ask the resident to attend the initial meeting (or rehearsal if there is an existing group) just to be an observer. Tell her she can bring a friend if that will make her feel more comfortable. If she attends but doesn't wish to stay, she should not be forced. However, usually she will!!!

CHAPTER FOUR

CONDUCTING A SUCCESSFUL DRAMA GROUP

Purpose of the Group

THE first meeting of the drama group should be devoted to a discussion on the meaning of drama in easy basic terms.

The purpose and goals of the group should also be discussed in a clear and concise manner. Stress the importance of participation in drama for fun rather than for expecting professional results. Martin Nolter, in the "Gerontologist," emphasizes that:

> "The objective should be maximum participation from all those involved, to create a cohesive group which will find physical and mental stimulation and pleasure in studying and creating drama."[1]

Discuss what the members wish to get out of the group. Talk about the kinds of scripts or shows the group wishes to present. New groups should begin with easy tasks such as discussion groups, poetry readings or dramatic/choral readings.

A simple questionnaire can be distributed to the members assessing their interests and own individual needs (see Appendix II).

Initial Meeting Time

Once the group is formed, it is important to set up a time and place to meet on a regular basis. Weekly meetings or rehearsals are

---
[1] Nolter, "Drama for the Elderly," p. 154.

most common, since continuity for the group is important. Rehearsal time should generally not exceed more than one hour in order to help keep the interest of the elderly members at a maximum.

Selection of a Show

With the group formed and rehearsals set, it is necessary to decide which show will be presented.

Many groups have found that musical shows seem to be the most appropriate not only to the participants but to the elderly audience as well. Music familiar to the aged makes it easier for them to relate to both as an actor and as an audience. Most groups feel the show chosen should not deal with physical violence.

As discussed earlier, a variety of dramatic forms and scripts are available. Although the type of script chosen should depend upon the nature of the group and the level and degree of their limitations, the drama coach should *not pick* the show for the group. Rather, he should help select a show of their choice. With the above in mind, a list of suggestions from the group can be drawn up. It is helpful to briefly discuss the story and plot of each suggested show with the members. The music, if any, can also be played by using a record or tape from the suggested show.

Any show to be done should be agreed upon by the majority of the members. Dissension among the members and dissatisfaction with the show will more than likely lead to an unsuccessful production. The group must feel comfortable and should enjoy the recreation experience of performing no matter what the show is. Don't be surprised if it takes one or two meetings to decide upon a show suitable for the group.

Adapting the Script

Once the show and script has been selected, the script must be written and adapted to meet the needs, limitations and abilities of the members. Remember, the script can be adapted to meet the needs of the group on almost any level.

No matter what script is used, the show should generally not last for more than an hour in length. Anything longer than this would probably create a problem since the attention span of the elderly may be limited. In addition, anything longer may be too tiring physically for the participants and may create problems in memorization of lines. Finally, the audience, especially if elderly, would probably also find it difficult to sit through if the show is more than an hour.

Once the script has been adapted, it should be typed on a large print typewriter in a clear and distinct manner. It is also not uncommon to find an aged person who is color blind. This can be overcome by using different colored inks, since some see certain colors better than others. For those who are totally blind, scripts should be put on tape. Individual coaching may also be helpful for the blind actor.

Auditioning

With the script adapted and in hand, the actors must be chosen to fill the parts of the play. This difficult step can be made easier through the process of auditioning. Although competition is a healthy aspect of team work, it is important not to create an environment conducive to jealousies or rivalries among the elderly actors. To keep the anxiety level of the actors at a minimum, I have found through experience that auditions (when appropriate) are the most democratic way of selecting the proper actor for the appropriate role.

Auditions also help take the drama coach *off the hook*. In my earlier years as a drama coach, I vividly remember how difficult it was choosing the resident I thought should play the leading role. Just think of all the problems this may cause and justifiably so!! "Why wasn't I picked?" "I'm just as good as her!" "Why should he get the leading role all the time?"

Auditioning gives every actor an equal opportunity to try for any part he desires. Since we are not professionals, auditions should be made as simple as possible. Any number of actors wishing to audition for a specific role can be asked to read certain lines from the particular part. A secret ballot with the names of those people auditioning for each part is given to the rest of the group. The group is asked to vote on the person they feel read the part the best. It should be stressed that those voting base their vote on the clarity, expression and feeling for which each part is read.

Although the group may aim for a high quality production, we must not forget that it is the reward of the recreation experience of the elderly actors which is the most important factor. Auditions foster a sense of fairness and team involvement among the participants of the group who democratically select the actor best suited for the role. Auditioning is also valuable in that it gives the actor a chance to stand before a group of people. Thus, the actor becomes less nervous and more at ease with the audience during a performance.

Rehearsals

Upon completion of auditions, the scripts should be underlined for each individual actor's role.

The first few rehearsals should be used as an orientation period for reading the script through by those who will be playing the roles. The actors should acquire an understanding of the characters they will be playing. They may sit in chairs on or below the stage to read through the script. Questions should be answered and comments discussed here to broaden the understanding of the play. Once the entire group has read through the script and everyone has a basis of the mood and tone of the show, rehearsals can begin with each act. Each act should be worked through until the primary actors have learned or memorized their lines (if memorization is required). Since the topic of memorization is a significant one, it will be dealt with separately in Chapter Five.

During rehearsals, the director should block each act. It is important for the elderly actor to get used to moving about and learning where to stand as early as possible. The more he does this, the quicker he will learn and remember.

Props and microphones should also be used as early as possible. Microphones can be camouflaged when possible but they should be used at any cost. Cordless microphones or those which fit around the neck are also helpful when available.

PRODUCTION AIDES

Although production aides need not always be elaborate, they do help enhance the drama production.

Costumes

Costumes can be as elaborate or as simple as you wish them to be. They do not have to be made in detail since most of the audience will be viewing them at a considerable distance from the stage. What is most important in costuming is to achieve the appropriate shape, flow or design of the costume to help identify the period and to set the mood of the play. It is also important to remember that whatever the costume, the aged person must be agile enough to wear or change his costume if necessary. Costumes must fit properly or they may inhibit the actor's performance. Utilizing costumes helps make the actor look more realistic as well as improving his performance, because he may feel more like the character he is playing.

Costumes can be made in accordance with the Occupational Therapy department or through the sewing class or arts and crafts class of the activities department. It may also be fun to involve families in helping to make costumes. Finally, the housekeeping department may be useful in acquiring old dresses, hats or outfits that can be used for costumes. Some groups add flowers, or lace to existing dresses, and others use old sheets to make their costumes.

Make-up

Make-up can also help to make the actor look more authentic and play his part with more feeling. One should be cautioned, however, not to overdo the make-up. It may also be necessary to check if anyone is allergic to make-up. Beards, wigs, and moustaches are often used to complement costumes and help achieve the required look for certain characters. The beautician or hair dresser of your facility may be able to help with the make-up.

Scenery

The mood and the period of a play can be achieved through the use of its set design and scenery in a few ways. First, one back drop can be used to depict the mood and period of the entire play. Second, set changes can be done but should be left simple and uncomplicated. The elderly actors must not feel uncomfortable *on the set*. The stage should not be cluttered but can be supplemented with wall

Figure 7. Simple costumes add to the authenticity of portraying characters in dramatic productions.

hangings, pictures on the walls or some minor props. Scenery can be painted on sheets or on scenery paper and hung on the rear wall of the stage.

As simple as a set may be, it is important to remember as David Welker points out:

"The set underlines or expresses the fundamental mood of the play . . . *mood* being used here to indicate all of the emotions which the playwright hopes to arouse in the audience as part of the experience of watching the play."[2]

---
[2]David Welker, *Theatrical Direction, The Basic Techniques* (Boston: Allyn and Bacon, Inc., 1971), p. 61.

In addition:

> "the set gives the audience information about the locale and period in which the play takes place and provides an effective esthetic experience for the audience."³

For more ideas on set design and costuming for certain shows, see Appendix IV.

Figure 8. Set design and simple props add to the success of the drama group productions.

---

³Ibid., p. 61.

CHAPTER FIVE

MEMORIZATION OF LINES

PERHAPS, one of the most commonly found and misunderstood problems among elderly drama groups is memorization of lines.

Memorization of lines has often been labeled by drama coaches, staff and participants themselves as inappropriate, impractical and almost impossible because of *old age*. Several factors seem to be responsible for this negative attitude which is important to discuss and hopefully alter.

Alex Comfort points out that:

> "Modern research indicates that a high proportion of the mental and attitudinal changes seen in "old" people are not biological effects of aging. They are the results of role playing. The trouble with the part we assign to "the old" is that it is a destructive part."[1]

Society, unfortunately assigns negative roles to the *aged* which have become stereotypical and difficult to change. These negative attitudes become a part of the elderly's own self image which are difficult to change until they can begin to see themselves in a different, more positive light.

Often, mandatory retirement ages are *imposed* on our aged population whether they are ready or willing to retire. Because they have reached a certain chronological age, they are supposed to play a role which society imposes on them. They have become *old* and are therefore branded less intelligent, often incapable and unable to function

---

[1]Comfort, *A Good Age*, p. 14.

within the role society has previously assigned them.

Prejudices and stereotypical traits have no boundaries. The *old* people of today's society, whether living independently or in a nursing home, bring with them their negative attitudes and demeaning self images. It is not surprising that many of those in nursing homes come to live out their remaining days as *useless old* people.

Part of our role as professionals within the field of leisure education and gerontology should be to help break down and reverse these negative stereotypical attitudes. Participation in worthwhile recreation activities such as a drama group is a beginning step for many. Further, memorization *is possible* and should be encouraged with old people. *Old dogs* can be taught new tricks. The more *new tricks* we can teach the elderly, the more we can help reverse their own self image and negative attitudes.

Although society paints a certain *negative* role for our aged population, we would be naive not to recognize that certain biological changes do take place with advancing age. One change which has been investigated is whether the primary problem in later life is the decline in learning or the decline in memory.

Memory Studies — Implications for Drama

In a memory study by J.G. Gilbert, two age groups (20-29 years and 60-69 years) whose performances on eleven tests were compared, found that although the older group performed more poorly, the extent of decline were different on all the tests. Gilbert's conclusion indicated that:

> "The aged decline was somewhat greater for delayed recall of information than for the immediate recall of it; performances were poorer later in the test session than they were soon after the information to be learned had been presented."[2]

According to Botwinick, this conclusion was challenged in a study by E.A. Jerome in 1959.

> "Though it is true older subjects showed a 54.6% deficit relative to the young . . . on the delayed recall of paired associates, it is important to note that they had a 58.7% deficit on immediate re-

---

[2] Jack Botwinick, *Aging and Behavior*, (New York: Springer Publishing Co., 1973, p. 255, quoting J.G. Gilbert, Memory loss in senescence, Journal of Abnormal and Social Psychology, 1941, pp. 73-86.

call of this materal. They may therefore have recalled less on the delayed test simply because they learned less during acquisition trials, but relative to what they had acquired, their delayed recall was superior to that of the young subjects."[3]

Jerome's conclusion indicated an age deficit in learning but not necessarily in retention.

In a test done by P.A. Moenster for short term retention, she used paragraphs of meaningful reading material instead of paired-associate words and tested people who ranged between 20 and 94 years of age. A multiple choice test of twenty questions was given immediately after the paragraph was read and approximately ten minutes later she gave the same test to measure memory. These results indicated that performances declined with age in both the learning and memory scores. However, when she tested for memory (taking into account an adjustment for the learning scores), there were no further age differences found. From this data, Botwinick also seemed to agree that "learning rather than short term memory, appears to be the problem in later life."[4]

A study done by Hulicka and Weiss also points to learning as the primary problem in later life and indicates how learning can set the limits for memory. Paired associates were given to elderly and younger subjects who were divided into sub-groups. Paired associate lists were given equally a number of times to each of the age sub-groups. To another sub-group of the elderly and young, the lists were given until they were learned. Another group of elderly were given training beyond the original learning limit. All the subjects were tested for recall of what they learned between five and twenty minutes after their learning. The younger group performed better in the learning and memory tests. However, the two groups were not significantly different in their memory scores when what they learned was taken into account. Thus, according to Botwinick, Hulicka and Weiss argued that what is remembered is dependent upon what is learned.

Other studies have shown that memory in later years does decline to some degree, regardless of how well or how much one has

---

[3]Botwinick, *Aging and Behavior*, p. 255 quoting E.A. Jerome, Age and learning, experimental studies, in J.E. Birren, *Handbook of Aging and the Individual*, (Chicago: University of Chicago Press, 1959), pp. 655-699.
[4]Botwinick, *Aging and Behavior*, p. 257.

learned. In spite of this, we can not ignore the fact that there is a significant relationship between what one learns and how much he remembers. It is obvious that if one does not learn, he will have little to recall or remember. If a participant in a drama group cannot learn his lines or script, he will obviously not be able to recall them later on.

Memorization Aides and Techniques

Several aides or techniques are available to help the elderly perform better. Many of these can be utilized to help the drama group participant learn lines and to increase performance abilities.

Some studies hypothesized that when learning a task involves organization of incoming information, the elderly did not perform as well as the young. D. Hultsch tested this hypothesis and found that out of three age groups, (young, middle, old), the oldest and middle age groups had the most trouble organizing their material. However, when specific instructions were given on how to organize their material, differences among the age groups were no longer found. This helped confirm the hypothesis that certain aged groups show poor performances partly because they are poor at organizing incoming information. However, as Botwinick noted, when helped in this area, they display a good ability to learn.

To facilitate a better performance with an elderly drama group, the director should help those learning their lines by giving specific instructions on how to organize and categorize their own individual parts.

Mediational techniques is another aid which, designed to highlight and associate, is used to help in acquiring and retaining new information or material.

A study by R.E. Canestrari found that "excellent, really extraordinary performances in paired-associate learning, may be seen when subjects are told to "form a mental picture" to connect each word-pair associate."[5]

These mediators may be verbal characteristics of visual imagery.

Hulicka and Grossman indicated that older people usually do not

---

[5]Botwinick, *Aging and Behavior*, p. 235, quoting R.E. Canestrari, Age changes in acquisition, G.A. Talland, *Human Aging and Behavior*, (New York: Academic Press, 1968), pp. 169-188.

use mediational techniques unless they are specifically instructed to do so. However, when given instructions on these techniques, they improve tremendously. They believed "part of the learning deficit observed in old . . . subjects . . . may be due to the failure to use mediational techniques spontaneously."[6]

It is suggested that the drama coach utilize mediational techniques as often as possible. Separate rehearsals can be set up to help with learning of lines. During these sessions, the director can teach and encourage the elderly actor to use verbal or visual mediators with associative techniques. Participants can be asked to draw a sketch that illustrates the words or meaning of a particular line being learned. Verbal mediators can be used by making a list of paired-associate words in certain lines. Canestrari gave subjects a task of paired-associate words. To help them learn the words better, a verbal mediator was given. For example, with the words "short" and "box," a short phrase that contained both words of the pair was provided and the word "a" was added to form the phrase "a short box." This can be utilized with any line or part which the elderly actor is having difficulty learning. These techniques help integrate material so it can be more easily managed.

Supportive Environment

Another important factor which affects how well the elderly actor will memorize or learn his lines is related in part to the *emotional context* or atmosphere in which the participant is placed during his learning process.

An important study points out that those aged who are placed under *evaluative situations*, and told that their performances will be compared to others, usually respond with stress and insecurity, making it more difficult to learn their lines. E. Ross, in a paired-associate learning study, gave three types of instruction: neutral, supportive, and challenging. The results showed that the performances of the elderly were best in the supportive situation and worst in the challenging ones. The supportive instruction included the important words, *your performance is NOT my main concern*. Thus, the

---

[6]Botwinick, *Aging and Behavior*, p. 235, quoting I. Hulicka and J. Grossman, Age-group comparisons for the use of mediators in a paired-associate learning. *Journal of Gerontology*, 1967, p. 22, pp. 46-51.

drama coach must aim toward creating a supportive atmosphere, continually supporting, praising and encouraging the members of the group. To eliminate a competitive atmosphere, the actors should never be compared to each other during rehearsals or in a performance. The emphasis should be placed on the importance of an enjoyable recreation experience rather than on the level of the dramatic performance achieved.

Interference

One of the most common explanations offered for a decline in learning and memory is that of interference. Psychologists explain that the learning process becomes blocked when other information or response sequences interrupt and disorganize on-going operations. This is commonly known as interference or retroaction. Interference may also be inferred when learning is interrupted because the person is doing more than one thing at a time or having two thoughts at the same time.

Interference holds important implications for the elderly drama group. Participants should be sure to learn their lines in a particular scene or act as well as possible before moving on to subsequent acts. This will help eliminate or keep to a minimum the problem of interference. They should also avoid doing more than one project at a time. If they are already involved in learning a part in one play, they should not be involved in another project which also requires learning of lines.

Other Helpful Hints

Scripts should be used as a *guide* for learning lines. Participants should be encouraged to use their own words, when learning lines, as long as the main thought is not changed.

Often, the drama participant is asked to play a part he has never done before or portray an emotion he may have difficulty doing. For example, in the play, "Fiddler on the Roof," an elderly actor who played the part of the policeman had to express his anger and break up the wedding of a Jewish couple. This was extremely difficult for him to do as he is the type of person who rarely expressed anger. In addition, being a fellow Jew, it was difficult to play the part of someone who disliked Jews. To help remove such an emotional block, he was asked to think back to his past, remembering something which angered him in real life. Ironically, he thought about the persecution of the Jewish people and became so angry he was more than able to express his anger during the rehearsal.

Finally, any kind of sensory, verbal or visual cues can be helpful in remembering lines. Props are especially important to use during rehearsals as they provide a visual image for the lines being learned. For example, in the show, "My Fair Lady," Henry Higgans asks Eliza Doolittle where his slippers are. Eliza, who is angry with him, is supposed to throw his slippers at him replying: "Here are your slippers." Giving the elderly actress, who is playing Eliza's part, an actual pair of slippers to throw will provide her with a sensory cue with which she can associate the line to be learned.

In summary, studies indicate that although elderly people may perform less well than younger people, they are certainly still capable of learning new material. The learning aides discussed here may be helpful in providing the elderly with techniques to improve their performances.

Figure 9. Members of senior citizen drama group successfully performing without the use of scripts.

CHAPTER SIX

THE ROLE OF THE DIRECTOR

A CRITICAL element to the success of the drama group is the role of the director. This role becomes a multi-faceted one, when directing an elderly drama group.

Creating a Positive Atmosphere

The director must create an atmosphere and environment conducive to a meaningful and enjoyable recreation experience. It is essential that the participants feel comfortable and at ease with themselves and the others in the group. A warm, friendly, manner will help establish a welcome feeling. In addition, the leader must be an enthusiastic one. A positive attitude, an enthusiastic approach, and a sincere manner will undoubtedly result in your acceptance as the drama coach or leader. Acceptance as the leader is crucial to maintaining control of the group.

Achieving Change

To achieve change or results in any group, the leader must be able to give orders which govern the behavior of its members. The word "orders" may seem strong. However, George Homans in his book, "The Human Group," describes "orders" as a word for giving directions, often informally by the leader of a small group. He uses the word because he feels:

"There is no single word that has just the right shade of meaning, and if we remember that an order in a group as in a formal organization, is a communication from the leader which governs the behavior of the members, we shall not get into trouble."[1]

It is important for the leader to be able to use his abilities, not as a complete authoritarian but as one who will facilitate a democratic approach, thereby establishing a climate for mutual respect and understanding among its members. In describing the growth of a drama group in a recreation center, one author discusses the role of the leader as follows:

> "In this first meeting, his task was also to win their acceptance as leader, as well as to demonstrate the character of their mutual relationship. He made it clear both by his words and actions that he and they were working together as active participants, not as passive pupils learning from a teacher. He likewise established his relationship to Mr. Edwards (a drama group participant, with a great need for acceptance) as one of cooperation, not rivalry."[2]

In furthering the development of mutual trust and cooperation, it is important for the leader to treat each of his members as an individual who matters. Be sure to greet them on an individual basis, using their names as you communicate. Often, rehearsals may begin with several members asking for your attention simultaneously. You can ask them to be patient, stressing that each one will have his question answered, individually. It is important to show that you notice and care about each one of them. Physical contact, as well as looking at someone when you talk, is important in building any human relationship. It is imperative to approach your members as equals on all levels, including an intellectual one.

The role of the director requires clear and concise directions to the drama participant. Clear instructions will remove fear from the members, making it easier to participate, thereby achieving better results in the final production. As Paula Gray in her book pointed out:

> "A good director is a strong director because he does not leave

---

[1] George C. Homans, *The Human Group*, (New York: Harcourt, Brace and World, Inc., 1950), p. 415.
[2] Susan H. Kubie and Gertrude Landau, *Group Work with the Aged*, (New York: Greenwood Press Publishers, 1953), p. 110.

actors, who have strong creative imaginations of their own, in doubt about what he means or intends; consequently, he takes great care to keep his directions clear so that the actors can easily accept not a dictatorship but an honest expression of opinion that can be supported and opened to discussion without generating fear and insecurity."[3]

Attitude of the Director

The success of the group is greatly dependent upon the attitude of the director and how he views the older person. We discussed earlier, how important it is for the elderly to believe in themselves and in their accomplishments. It is essential for the director to communicate his belief in the capabilities of each member of the group. What we expect of the older person, is how they will behave. If we expect them to fail, they will. If we expect them to succeed, they will. Praise and encouragement by the director must be communicated on a consistent basis to every member. A non-judgmental climate should be created, allowing for the acceptance of suggestions, opinions and responses without being right or wrong. A sentiment I have often heard from the members of my own drama group is: "No matter what we do or how we do it, you always seem to praise and encourage us. You make us feel good and give us the courage to continue even when we doubt ourselves."

In addition to creating and maintaining a cohesive, smooth functioning group, it is the director's responsibility to deal with the play itself and the individual performances of his actors. He should have a basic understanding of the play and an awareness of the talents and capabilities of his participants regarding their voices, intellectual abilities and any physical limitations. He may also need to rewrite or adapt the script to meet the needs of the elderly group.

Dealing with Health Problems

Another important element to a successful production, is the ability of the director to deal with certain intrinsic health problems

---

[3]Paula Gray, *Dramatics for the Elderly*, (New York: Teachers College Press, 1974), p. 36, quoting Francis Hodge, *Play Directing and Analysis, Communication and Style*, (Englewood Cliffs, New Jersey: Prentice-Hall, Inc., 1971), p. 70.

which may be encountered with the elderly drama participant. In the same survey taken by the author, certain health problems related to the members were also cited. The following table exhibits some of these problems and their implications and offers some techniques the director may use as possible solutions. Paula Gray points out that some of these problems which she cites as physical and psychological limitations also seem to have hindered the establishment of drama groups in senior centers and residential care settings.

Table II
DEALING WITH HEALTH PROBLEMS OF THE DRAMA PARTICIPANT

Problem:	Implications:	Suggested Techniques:
Poor Vision	Can affect reading of script.	Large print type or hand printed script. Underline each script with colored ink.
	Can affect learning of lines.	Use tape recorder. Utilize individual coaching.
	Difficulty in entering or leaving stage.	Be sure to block each act. Use minimal physical movement. Give specific instructions as to where to enter and leave stage area.
	Difficulty in blocking on stage.	Place colored tape on floor. Keep visually impaired actor near center stage, close to prompter.
Poor Vision		Use small flash light to tell actor when to speak. Remind actors to wear glasses. Use large print cue cards.
Poor Hearing	Difficulty in understanding cues on stage.	Place actor and face him near prompter when possible.

Table II (Cont'd.)

Problem:	Implications:	Suggested Techniques:
		Write cues on props when appropriate.
		Use microphones, which help actors and audience. Also helps other actors in show hear those talking on stage.
		Remind actors to speak loud and clear.
Poor Hearing		Remind and encourage those who wear hearing aides to do so.
Immobility Non Ambulatory Participants	Difficulty in moving around on stage.	Minimize moving of actors in wheel chairs.
		Place on stage in position before curtain opens.
		Direct others around wheel chair.
		Camouflage wheel chair with props or scenery when appropriate.
		Use ramps for stage entrance and exit when available.
Heart Problems CVA Arthritis Poor Gait	Limited movements on and off stage area.	Use chairs when appropriate. Limit standing of actors. Limit entrances and exits. Utilize fellow actors to help others on stage. Have staff or volunteers assist with entrance and exits.

Table II (Cont'd.)

Problem:	Implications:	Suggested Techniques:
Reading Difficulty	Reading difficulty may be due to illiteracy, language barrier or aphasia.	Private coaching. Transcribe script onto tape. Transliterate script into appropriate language when possible. Use others who may know the appropriate second language. Improvise scripts. Minimize lines when possible.

Dealing with Personality Problems

Some problems may be anticipated while others may not. The director must be prepared to handle any problem, especially those which may appear unexpectedly within the group. Because individual needs are satisfied on many different levels, various behavior patterns may become evident as the drama group progresses. Often, we begin to see those who are hesitant to participate actively, those who are assertive and wish to take over, those who are always negative and those whose self confidence is so great they rarely listen to others, including the director. Ann Thurman and Carole Piggans in their book, Drama Activities with the Older Adult, discuss some of the following behavior and personality problems which may affect the drama group.

The Passive Participant. Playing a new role, be it in a dramatic show, or in a real life situation, is sometimes a difficult task. Many participants of elderly drama groups, come from a background whose roles differ from those of today. The woman's role which was primarily raising her family, left little time for play. The role of the adult excluded *having fun* or enjoying structured recreation experiences such as drama. Thus, as Thurman and Piggans point out, some seniors will join the drama group but will hesitate in becoming actively involved. It therefore becomes the responsibility of the director to help break the barriers of the past roles, allowing the elderly not only to participate in the group but to accept a different role, enjoying a new recreation experience. Through acceptance of drama as a valuable experience, the older person may begin to participate on a more active level, allowing himself to *fantasize, make believe,* or *play*.

The atmosphere created by the director is an important catalyst in encouraging active participation in a more free, out-going way. It is also important to foster a feeling of acceptance among the group to help eliminate fear of ridicule or competition. Some members may be more self conscious than others and will respond more actively when less pressure is exerted upon them. In this case, the director should address the entire group, rather than single out any one particular member.

It is also important for the director to be able to relate to the group on the same level. Relaying a personal story to the group, or admitting a mistake, will help put the members at ease, allowing them to see the leader in a more human light.

The Assertive Participant. The old expression, "there is always one in the crowd," probably holds true for every type of group. The advantage for the director in dealing with the assertive participant, is that he is easily detected. He will probably talk out of turn, always trying to be in control, including making decisions for everyone in the group.

The director needs a great deal of patience in dealing with this type of personality. One method is to acknowledge the *boss's* idea, while at the same time explain that it is the group's decision which needs to be adhered to. You can also acknowledge how valuable his idea is to the group, but remind him that there are others who need to be considered.

The *assertive participant* has a special need to be recognized. The director can help channel this need through a more constructive path by giving him other responsibilities within the group. He may wish to set up chairs, take attendance or prepare microphones for rehearsals. Using the *boss's* energy in a constructive, satisfying manner will reward the participant as well as the director and group.

The Negative Participant. The negative personality, whether indirectly or not, always seems to *put down* or dampen a particular situation. Comments such as "Oh, that will never work," or "We shouldn't be doing it this way," are typical of the negative person.

Constant reassurance and encouragement is one way of handling the negative person. "Let's try it, even if it may not work," is one way of getting the negative participant to join in. The results will probably be positive, reinforcing the fact that something can work. Involvement, regardless of a negative mood, is important to the participant and to the entire group.

The Director as Producer

In many cases, the role of the director includes producing and coordinating the technical aspects of the production as well.

It is often the director's job to coordinate performance dates and the use of facilities within his agency. He is often needed to coordinate production crews who are responsible for costumes, make-up, scenery, props and lighting. He will also need to arrange publicity as well as programs and tickets if necessary.

The final production will be the result of painstaking efforts in both directing and producing with the elderly drama group.

Humor and the Director

Humor is a part of life and should have an important role within the drama group. It is up to the director to create an environment which lends itself to humorous situations which may occur. The director must help make the members feel comfortable enough to be able to laugh at one's mistakes with the group.

I can recall a situation in a rehearsal of "Fiddler on the Roof" which brought humor to us all. During the wedding scene, Motel the tailor was supposed to put an imaginary ring on his bride's finger. During this particular rehearsal, I noticed eighty-five year old, Mr. K., placing a real gold ring around his bride's finger. When I asked why and where he got a real gold ring, his eighty-year old leading lady replied: "I made him buy it, that's where he got it . . . You didn't think I would marry a poor tailor without a real gold ring, did you??" There was little I could do but finish rehearsing the scene. Our pair became officially engaged but unfortunately never married!!

CHAPTER SEVEN

INTEGRATING DRAMA WITH OTHER PROGRAM AREAS

ONE of the most valued benefits of drama is its unique ability to integrate itself with so many different recreational forms.

The use of arts and crafts may be integrated into drama to help complement the group's production. Crafts can be utilized in costume making, prop construction, painting scenery and backdrops. Puppetry also depends heavily upon arts and crafts. The use of crafts also provides an additional outlet and program area for those who do not wish to act but enjoy participating in the drama group.

Music as a universal language, helps create the proper mood and sets the tone for the drama group production. It is often used to introduce the play itself through a musical synopsis of medleys from the show being presented. It also helps introduce or signify the beginning of a particular act as well as the change of scenes between acts. Finally, music enhances those elderly productions which utilize a chorus and offer still another area of involvement for those who do not wish to be singled out on stage.

Dance is another art form which lends itself so importantly to drama. It affords those oldsters who enjoy dancing, an additional means of participation in certain shows. Dance movements and exercises are also useful in maintaining physical fitness of the elder participant. Finally, certain shows, such as the ballet, could not be done without dance.

The integration of drama as an educational experience is also important to recognize. Learning lines, and providing mental stimulation by keeping the mind active, helps achieve increased levels of attention spans. Drama also increases one's knowledge as to the various dramatic forms and scripts and allows for appreciation of theatre and performances one may not have been previously able to share. Drama as an educational experience also helps foster group awareness and teaches the elder participant the need for group cooperation and cohesiveness.

Drama as a social activity is another facet to be offered. Participants are given the chance to establish new peer group relationships as well as to provide entertainment to its audience on a social nature.

All of these elements can be considered the spokes of a wheel which help form the hub or nucleus of dramatics as a recreation activity. Regardless of the type of drama being performed, success is more than likely to occur. A professional director is *not* essential to the elderly drama group. What *is* necessary is a recreation leader whose own creativity, positive attitude and innovative approach will allow his participants to utilize their maximum abilities and talents under the best possible conditions. The combination of all of these elements will help provide an activity which will enrich the lives of the drama participant for many years to come.

APPENDIX I

THIS THEY CALL A CHICKEN?

(An Original Comedy)
F RED G REENBLATT

THE CAST

Sadie Schwartz:	An elderly resident of the Sunnybrook Nursing Home who always seems to be complaining about something, especially the food.
Annie Greenstein:	An elderly resident of the Sunnybrook Nursing Home.
Sophie Brown:	An elderly resident with a positive outlook.
Sarah Daniels:	A new tablemate.
Waitress:	A pleasant, helpful woman who shows genuine concern for the residents of the home.
Drama coach:	A younger gentleman who conducts the Sunnybrook Chorus and Players. (The real drama coach or recreation leader can play this part if necessary.)
Piano player:	A resident of the home.

ACT I

(IN THE DINING ROOM OF THE SUNNYBROOK NURSING HOME)
(ON STAGE: Sadie Schwartz, Annie Greenstein, Sophie Brown)

SADIE: You know, I've had it with this food already! Every

Appendix I

	day it's the same food!! It's either chicken with potatoes or potatoes with chicken! And it's never cooked the way I like it!
ANNIE:	Sadie, what do you want? You think they can cook the way every single resident likes to eat? Be happy you have a place to get a good meal!!
SADIE:	Oy, please, you call this a good meal! I'm sending this chicken back. Waitress!! Waitress!! New, what takes her so long?

(WAITRESS ENTERS)

WAITRESS:	Yes, Mrs. Schwartz. What can I do for you?
SADIE:	First, you can tell me what takes you so long when I call?
WAITRESS:	I'm sorry, Mrs. Schwartz, but I do have other residents to serve as well.
SADIE:	Look at this!! This—you call a chicken??
	(Sadie holds up chicken)
	This is no chicken . . . This is a rooster!! And it's not even cooked. Look at these black lines. It must be from fighting with other chickens.
WAITRESS:	Calm down, Mrs. Schwartz. If you don't like this piece of chicken, I'll bring you another.
ANNIE:	Why not. She's already gone through four chickens today!
SADIE:	Well, it better be here before lunch tomorrow!!

(WAITRESS LEAVES)

SOPHIE:	You know, Sadie, you don't have to be so short tempered with our waitress. She is only trying to do her job and I might add, she does a good one at that.
SADIE:	Oy . . . another county heard from!
SOPHIE:	Well, It's true!! You know, I've only been here for a few months and I've never heard you do anything but complain.
SADIE:	So what else is there to do when you're old?
SOPHIE:	Well, I don't know about you, but I've found some

SADIE:	very interesting and worthwhile things to do here. Like what?
SOPHIE:	I volunteer two days a week as a librarian in the home. I'm a floor captain with the resident council and I attend all the activities here. I love the cooking class.
SADIE:	New, if you love it so much, why don't *you* cook our meals. Maybe we'll get chicken instead of rooster.
ANNIE:	You know, Sadie, Sophie is right. Maybe if you did something to occupy your time, you'd feel better. Why don't you join the drama group with me? I attend every week and we are rehearsing for a show right now. You might like it. Come with me tomorrow.
SADIE:	Oy please, me an actress? I have no talent.
ANNIE:	You'd be surprised. That's what I thought before I joined.
SADIE:	I'm too sick. I can't.
ANNIE:	Oh stop complaining already. It's time to start thinking positive. No one says it's easy Sadie, but you have to begin believing in yourself. (An original song can be written and sung here with the chorus. The song should be one with a positive outlook.)
SADIE:	Well, maybe I'll come with you, but I'll just watch.

(CURTAIN CLOSES)

ACT II

(IN THE AUDITORIUM
OF THE SUNNYBROOK NURSING HOME)

(THE DRAMA GROUP IS REHEARSING)

NARRATOR: It took some convincing. But it looks like Mrs. Schwartz has agreed to join the drama group—at least as an observer.

(CURTAIN OPENS)

(THE DRAMA GROUP IS ABOUT TO REHEARSE PART OF THE SHOW WHICH WILL BE PRESENTED IN ACT IV)

DRAMA COACH: Good afternoon everyone. How are you today? We have a lot of work today. Our show is only a week away. I would like to remind everyone to let me know how many of your guests will be attending opening night of our show here at the home. Please don't forget we will be doing the show three times. I will have a written schedule for you tomorrow. Before we begin today, I would like to introduce a newcomer to our group. I know it's a little late in rehearsals but Mrs. Schwartz is a friend of Annie Greenstein's and she would like to sit in as a member of the chorus.

SADIE: Hello. Thank you for accepting me so late into the drama group. I think I would just like to watch today, if you don't mind.

COACH: That's fine. Why don't you sit next to your friend Annie. If you wish you can sing along with the chorus.

SADIE: Okay, but you know I am not an actress. I don't know how well I can sing either.

COACH: Don't worry, Mrs. Schwartz. Just do the best you can and follow along with the chorus.

SADIE: Okay, thank you.

COACH: We don't have much time today, so I would like to just go over one or two songs.

PIANIST: (THE PIANO PLAYER BEGINS TO PLAY THE WRONG SONG)

ANNIE: That's the wrong song. That's not the song we've been rehearsing in our show.

PIANIST: Just a second!! Mrs. Greenstein, there is only one director here and that is our drama coach. So don't tell me what to do!

COACH: Ladies, Ladies!! Please. Mrs. Samuels our piano player is right. You know there can only be one director. Please let me handle this.

PIANIST: Thank you coach. I'm sorry if I played the wrong song. I remember which song to play now.

COACH: That's okay, Mrs. Samuels. Take your time and let's try it one more time.
(THE PIANIST PLAYS THE RIGHT SONG AND THE CHORUS SINGS A SONG FROM THE SHOW THEY ARE REHEARSING FOR ACT IV).

COACH: That was excellent, chorus. And Mrs. Schwartz, you were also terrific. I heard you very clearly among all of the chorus members. You have a very nice voice.

SADIE: Oh, thank you. Do you really mean it?

COACH: Yes, it was really very good. Well, that's it for today. I will see you all at dress rehearsal. Thank you and have a good day.

(CURTAIN CLOSES)

ACT III

(BACK IN THE DINING ROOM
OF THE SUNNYBROOK NURSING HOME)
(ON STAGE: — SITTING AT TABLE — SADIE SCHWARTZ, ANNIE GREENSTEIN AND SOPHIE BROWN)

NARRATOR: It seems as if Sadie may have even enjoyed participating in the drama group. Let's see if her friends can convince here to continue with the group.

(CURTAIN OPENS)

ANNIE: Good morning, Sadie. Well, how did you like the drama group?

SADIE: It was okay for the first time. But I really don't know if I will continue. I don't feel so good, you know.

SOPHIE: I knew it! It was too good to be true. One meal without complaining. So what's wrong today, Sadie?

SADIE: Oy, the usual . . . my head hurts, my legs are no good, my arthritis is bothering me and I can't see.

SOPHIE: So why don't you go to see the doctor?

SADIE: Oh, I will, as soon as I feel better.

ANNIE: You know Sadie, maybe you'd feel better if you found

	yourself a friend.
SADIE:	But I have friends.
ANNIE:	No . . . you know what kind of friend I mean!
SADIE:	You mean???
ANNIE:	Yes, I mean a male friend!!
SADIE:	What??? A male friend?? Please, I have enough trouble already, and besides even if I had a male friend, what would we do? Where would we go???
ANNIE:	Oh, that's easy enough. You can stay right here in the home or you can do what Harry and I used to do.
SADIE:	And what's that?
ANNIE:	We borrowed our children's house for a day!!
SADIE:	That sounds great. Except with my legs and my eyes I can't leave the home.
SOPHIE:	Well, that's true Sadie. You know, maybe you'd better stick to joining the drama group for your fun!
SADIE:	I think you're right. You know my children were here yesterday. My daughter told me that if I stuck to the drama group, she would take me out for a delicious dinner. I think I'll even ask for a bigger part. Who knows, maybe I'll be a star and become famous. I understand the television and newspapers may be here for our show.

ACT IV

(THE AUDITORIUM OF THE SUNNYBROOK NURSING HOME)

NARRATOR: The big day has arrived. The Sunnybrook Chorus and players are proud to present their musical revue and salute to the Broadway theatre.

(AT THIS POINT YOU CAN WRITE YOUR OWN SHOW TO BE PRESENTED AS ACT IV)

SOME SUGGESTIONS FOR A SHOW
TO BE PRESENTED MAY BE:

A musical revue of Broadway theatre.
Short scenes of Broadway shows with musical numbers.

A vaudeville talent show.
A musical adaptation of a Broadway show or an adaptation of an existing play.

ACT V

(IN THE DINING ROOM
OF THE SUNNYBROOK NURSING HOME)

(SITTING AT THE DINING ROOM TABLE, A NEW RESIDENT IS PRESENT)

(ON STAGE: Sadie Schwartz, Annie Greenstein, Sophie Brown and New Resident — Sarah Daniels)

NARRATOR: The show was a smashing success. And so was Sadie!! Let's see how Sadie is able to handle her fame and succcess.

(CURTAIN OPENS)

SOPHIE: Sadie, you were absolutely terrific in the show. We didn't know you had it in you.

SADIE: Neither did I. And I loved every minute of it. Why did I wait so long to join the drama group?

ANNIE: Sadie, you outdid yourself. Can I have your autograph? And just think, you're going to be in the newspapers and on television. You really are a star!!

SADIE: Oh thank you ladies. Boy, do I have something to tell you all. You won't believe this. My children were here for the show and they kept their promise. They took me out to dinner to this really fancy schmancy restaurant after the show. And guess what? The food was terrible!! And worst of all, the chicken wasn't even cooked!! It had black lines. I couldn't believe it!! You know ladies, the food HERE really isn't so bad!!

SARAH: *The food here isn't so bad!!!*

SOPHIE: Oh, by the way, Sadie, I'd like you to meet our new table mate, Sarah Daniels.

SADIE: How do you do, Mrs.... Mrs. Daniels? How are you?

Appendix I 55

SARAH: How am I? Oy, don't ask. I've only been here for three days and already I've had my table changed three times. I feel like I'm on a merry-go-round. I gave up my apartment to come here. I gave up my furniture. And I just got a slip from the clinic…NOW THEY WANT MY BLOOD TOO!!!

SADIE: Oh, I'm sorry.

SARAH: You're sorry? Well…I've had it here and I've had it with this food. THIS THEY CALL A CHICKEN????
     (HOLDS UP CHICKEN)
THIS IS NO CHICKEN…THIS IS A ROOSTER!!!

(CURTAIN CLOSES)

APPENDIX II

DRAMA GROUP ASSESSMENT AND INTEREST QUESTIONNAIRE

Participant's Name: _____
1. Can you sing?   Yes _____ No _____
2. Have you ever had voice training or voice lessons?
                                    Yes _____ No _____
3. What type of songs do you like to sing?
   _____
   _____

4. Can you dance?   Yes _____ No _____
5. What type of dance do you like to do?
   Waltz _____ Fox Trot _____ Tango _____
   Mombo _____ Rumba _____ Cha Cha _____
   Lindy _____ Other _____
6. Do you play a musical instrument?
                                    Yes _____ No _____
7. Which musical instrument do you play?
   _____

8. Can you read music?   Yes _____ No _____
9. Do you have any artistic abilities? Yes _____ No _____
10. What artistic abilities do you have?
    _____
    _____

Appendix II

11. Can you paint or draw?   Yes _____   No _____
12. What type of drawing do you enjoy most?
    Oil painting _____ Scenery _____ Posters _____
13. Have you ever acted before?   Yes _____   No _____
    If yes, where _____
14. Please list below the parts you have played:
    Role   Show:
    _____
    _____

15. We would like to know which jobs you have done in a drama group or what you might like to do in the group now. Please complete the following questions.

JOB:	HAVE DONE:	WOULD LIKE TO DO:
Assistant Director		
Set Designer		
Scenery Painting		
Lighting		
Sound		
Ushering		
Publicity		
Stage props		
Costume making		
Stage Hand		
Other		

APPENDIX III

DRAMA SURVEY

1. How often does your drama group meet?
   Weekly _____ Bi-Weekly _____ Monthly _____ Other _____
2. How long does each meeting or rehearsal usually last?
   ½ hour _____ 1 hour _____ 1 ½ hour _____ Other _____
3. What is the average length of time you usually spend preparing or rehearsing for a show or play?
   1-2 months _____ 2-4 months _____ Other _____
4. What is the nature of the participants in your drama group?
   Skilled nursing residents   _____
   Health related residents   _____
   Community seniors   _____
   Day care participants   _____
   Other   _____
5. On the *Left* side of the page please check which components you feel were essential in setting up your drama group. If you are the director of an *existing* drama group, indicate which components you think would have been necessary.
   On the *Right* side of the page, briefly describe the way in which you would obtain these components.

PROBLEM: **SOLUTION**

__ Drama coach   _____
                                        _____
                                        _____

___ Basic knowledge of dramatics

___ Appropriate dramatic material

___ Adequate funds or budget

___ Adequate interest of participant

___ Support of administration

___ Staff cooperation

___ Adequate supplies available

___ Proper facilities available

___ Adequate space

___ Other _____

6. Please check any of the problems listed below which may have been expressed by your participants as reasons for not being able to or not wishing to participate in the drama group.

PROBLEM:	NEVER	SOME-TIMES	FRE-QUENTLY	ALWAYS
Too old				
Physically disabled				
I can't memorize				

I can't act
I can't sing
I never did this before
Other reasons: _____
_____

7. What percentage of the participants in your drama group have never acted or had any kind of dramatic experience BEFORE they joined your group? ____%
8. On the *Left* side of the page, please check any of the problems listed below, which you may have had to deal with while conducting the drama group.

   On the *Right* side of the page, briefly describe how you helped solve each problem.

PROBLEM: **SOLUTION:**

__ Impaired vision

__ Impaired hearing

__ Immobility
(wheel chair, poor gait, etc.)
__ Speech impairment

__ Inability to read

__ Memorization problem

__ Forgetfulness

__ No self confidence

__ Other _____
_____

9. Please check the frequency with which you may have used any of the dramatic forms listed below:

DRAMATIC FORM:	NEVER USED	SOMETIMES	FREQUENTLY
Original script	_____	_____	_____
Dramatic reading	_____	_____	_____
Existing script or adaptation of existing script	_____	_____	_____
Pantomime	_____	_____	_____
Pageant	_____	_____	_____
Puppet show	_____	_____	_____
Fashion show	_____	_____	_____
Improvisation	_____	_____	_____
Other: _____	_____	_____	_____

10. Do you ever use children or younger adults in your drama productions? Yes _____ No _____
    If so, where do the children come from? _____

11. Have you ever cast an older member in the role of a younger person? Yes _____ No _____
    If not, please explain why. _____

12. Have you ever cast a female as a male?
    Yes _____ No _____
    If not, please explain why. _____

13. Have you ever cast a male as a female?
    Yes _____ No _____
    If not, please explain why. _____

14. How often do you use a chorus in your shows or in your dramatic productions?
    Never _____ Sometimes _____ Frequently _____ Always _____

15. How often do you use a narrator in your shows or productions?
    Never _____ Sometimes _____ Frequently _____ Always _____
16. How often do you require your participants to memorize lines?
    Never _____ Sometimes _____ Frequently _____ Always _____
17. What percentage of the participants in your drama group have been able to memorize their lines adequately enough for your productions? _____ %
18. Please check the frequency with which you may have used any of the techniques listed below to help your participants memorize their lines.

TECHNIQUE:	NEVER USED	SOME-TIMES	FRE-QUENTLY
Use their own words	_____	_____	_____
Action Association (accompany lines said with a specific action)	_____	_____	_____
Sensory Recall (remembering a past action to help you feel a similar emotion)	_____	_____	_____
Rote learning	_____	_____	_____
Tape recording	_____	_____	_____
Individual coaching	_____	_____	_____
Cue cards	_____	_____	_____
Other: _____	_____	_____	_____

19. Please check the frequency with which you have used any of the following during your dramatic productions.

	NEVER	SOME-TIMES	FRE-QUENTLY	ALWAYS
Costumes	_____	_____	_____	_____
Scenery	_____	_____	_____	_____
Props	_____	_____	_____	_____
Programs	_____	_____	_____	_____
Publicity	_____	_____	_____	_____
Microphones	_____	_____	_____	_____
Cue cards	_____	_____	_____	_____

Piano player
Records and/or tapes
Other: _____

20. Where do you get costumes? _____

21. Do you ever have residents help make costumes?
    Yes _____ No _____

22. Who is responsible for the scenery in your productions? _____

23. Who is usually responsible for the lights, curtains, etc. of your production? _____

24. Please list below any benefits or values you feel may result from participating in a drama group.

25. What percentage of participants do you feel have changed their attitudes toward themselves *AFTER* participating in your drama group? _____ %

APPENDIX IV

SUGGESTED MATERIALS
FOR ELDERLY DRAMA GROUPS

MUSICALS:	SCENERY SUGGESTED:	COSTUMES SUGGESTED:
Fiddler on the Roof	Backdrop of Fiddler on a small house. Painting of other houses in the village. Chuppa for wedding scene can be made of four poles covered with cardboard and decorated with flowers or leaves.	Long skirts or dresses of the period. Shawls for the ladies can also be worn. Suits for the men with vests. No jackets.
My Fair Lady	Inside of Higgans House — chairs, table, lamp, pictures on the wall. At the races — Fences made of poster board. Scene of grandstands in background.	Long dresses of the period. Formal suits for men with top hats.
South Pacific	Backdrop of island with water and boat.	Sailor outfits or T-shirts with an anchor

Outdoor shower can be made of large box or carton. Cover box with weeds. drawn on them for the men.

OTHER SUGGESTED MUSICALS

Showboat
Oklahoma
Annie Get Your Gun
The Music Man
Carousel
The King and I
Camelot

ORIGINAL SCRIPTS

A day in the Nursing Home.
A bingo game.
Dating at eighty.
The Roommate Dilemma.

BIBLIOGRAPHY

1. Adams, Ronald. Games, Sports and Exercises for the Physically Handicapped. 2nd ed. Philadelphia: Lea and Febiger, 1975.
2. Avedon, Elliot. Therapeutic Recreation Services. Englewood Cliffs: Prentice-Hall, 1974.
3. Botwinick, Jack. Aging and Behavior. New York: Springer, 1973.
4. Carlson, R.E., Deppe, T.R. and Maclean, J.R. Recreation in American Life, 2nd ed. Belmont: Wadsworth, 1972.
5. Carlson, R.E., Deppe, T.R. and Peterson, J.A. Recreation and Leisure — The Changing Scene, 3rd ed. Belmont: Wadsworth, 1979. 220-226.
6. Comfort, Alex. A Good Age. New York: Crown, 1976.
7. Corbin, Dan H. Recreation Leadership. Englewood Cliffs: Prentice-Hall, 1970. 201-213.
8. Danford, Howard H. Creative Leadership in Recreation. Boston: Allyn and Bacon, 1964.
9. Farrell, Patricia and Lundergren, Herberta. The Process of Recreation Programming — Theory and Technique. New York: Wiley, 1978.
10. Frye, Virginia Mary. Therapeutic Recreation — Theory, Philosophy and Practice. Harrisburg: Stackpole, 1972.
11. Gray, Paula Gross. Dramatics for the Elderly. New York: Teachers College Press, 1974.
12. Hodge, Francis. Play Directing Analysis, Communication and Style. Englewood Cliffs: Prentice-Hall, 1971.
13. Homans, George C. The Human Group. New York: Harcourt, Brace and World, 1950.
14. Kraus, Richard. Recreation Today, Program Planning and Leadership. New York: Meredith, 1966. 181-195.
15. Kraus, Richard; Carpenter, Gary; and Bates, Barbara. Recreation Leadership and Supervision. 2nd ed. New York: CBS College, 1981. 105-107.
16. Kraus, Richard. Recreation Leaders Handbook. New York: McGraw-Hill, 1955. 222-245.
17. Kubie, Susan H. and Landau, Gertrude. Group Work with the Aged. New York: Greenwood Press, 1953. 105-125.
18. Lindner, Caplow Erna; Harpaz, Leah; and Samberg, Sonya. Therapeutic

Dance Movement. New York: Human Sciences Press, 1979.
19. Nolter, Martin. "Drama for the Elderly: They Can Do It." The Gerontologist, Vol 13, no. 2 (Summer, 1973): 153-157.
20. Shivers, Jay S. and Fait, Hollis F. Recreational Service for the Aging. Philadelphia: Lea and Febiger, 1980. 137-144. 158-165.
21. Telander, Maurice; Quinlan, Flora; and Verson, Karol. Acting Up. Chicago: Coach House, 1982.
22. Thurman, Ann H. and Piggans, Carol Ann. "Dramatic Activities with Older Adults: A Handbook for Leaders." Activities, Adaptation and Aging. Vol 2 nos. 2/3 Winter/Spring, 1982.
23. Vannier, Maryellen. Recreation Leadership. Philadelphia: Lea and Febiger, 1977. 113-128.
24. Waitley, Dennis E. The Psychology of Winning. Tape no. 3, Chicago: Nightingale Conant Corp., 1978.
25. Weiskopf, Donald C. A Guide to Recreation and Leisure. Boston: Allyn and Bacon, 1975. 239-242.
26. Welker, David. Theatrical Direction — The Basic Techniques. Boston: Allyn and Bacon, 1971.

TY LIBRARY

on as you